Making
Little League
BASEBALL®
More Fun for Kids

30 Games and Drills Guaranteed to Improve Skills and Attitudes

Randy Voorhees

New York   Chicago   San Francisco   Lisbon   London   Madrid   Mexico City
Milan   New Delhi   San Juan   Seoul   Singapore   Sydney   Toronto

Library of Congress Cataloging-in-Publication Data

Voorhees, Randy.
    Making little league baseball more fun for kids : 30 games and drills guaranteed to
improve skills and attitudes / Randy Voorhees.
        p.   cm.
    ISBN 0-07-138560-6
    1. Little league baseball.   I. Title.

    GV880.5 .V66   2002
    796.357'62—dc21   2002023797

8 9 10 11 12 13 14 15 16 17 18 19 20 21 22 23 DOC/DOC 0 9 8

ISBN-13: 978-0-07-138560-2
ISBN-10:   0-07-138560-6

Cover and interior design by Nick Panos
Cover photographs copyright © Image Club Graphics

McGraw-Hill books are available at special quantity discounts to use as premiums and
sales promotions, or for use in corporate training programs. For more information, please
write to the Director of Special Sales, Professional Publishing, McGraw-Hill, Two Penn
Plaza, New York, NY 10121-2298. Or contact your local bookstore.

This book is printed on acid-free paper.

*This book is dedicated to my Little League coach,
Howard "Bubby" Gailloux, and to the memory of the late,
great Herman "Champ" Clark.*

Contents

Contents

Acknowledgments

My sincere thanks to all the baseball coaches in my life, including Bubby Gailloux, Joe Carbone, Champ Clark, Lou Cioppi, Hank DeSimone, John Monteleone, and Butch Miller.

Special thanks to John Monteleone, for letting me write this book, and to my friend Mark Gola for helping me with the writing and the photography.

An additional thanks to Michael Plunkett, photographer; Lance Van Auken, director of media relations at Little League Baseball; the Ewing Township Little League for use of their field; coach Mike Coryell for his help and participation in the photography shoot; and all the Little League players (models) who spent a hot summer morning out on the ball field—Bryan Bleakley, Ben Caiola, Travis Carroll, Ryan Coryell, Ajani Counts, Bradley DeUmberto, Andrew Dickinson, Anthony Freda, and Jimmy and Alex Wishbow.

Last, thanks to Rob Taylor, my editor, for believing in the concept.

Introduction

As I was growing up in Lambertville, New Jersey, nothing could grab my attention faster than a baseball game, whether it was an organized event or one played out on the sandlot. From the time we loosened our arms until the time the final out was nestled in someone's glove, my senses were tuned to every sound, smell, and feel of the game. I loved baseball then, and I love it now.

I often reflect on those early days, and at times I even catch myself daydreaming about some play that happened 30 years ago on some nondescript vacant lot. It is those childhood experiences, along with my present-day coaching experience, that motivated me to write this book. Playing and coaching the game of baseball is fun.

I believe that coaches should take to heart the words *game* and *fun*. They are the essence of baseball. Kids don't join Little League teams to be coached by us, as important as we may be. They join to play a fun game with their friends. That is indisputably their motivation. Therefore, if we focus on the game itself and how to make it more fun, we'll keep more kids involved longer, and they'll improve as people and players.

Making Little League Baseball More Fun for Kids includes 30 games-within-the-game that you can play during practice sessions.

Many of the games can be played at home; others are designed to involve the entire team. Each of the games is fun and simple to coordinate; all of them teach or refine essential baseball skills. I believe that by playing these games kids will enjoy their practice time more, while improving their technique.

I have visited many Little League practices and watched kids participate in drill after drill after drill. I understand that drills play a role in developing players' skills and that youth coaches are doing what they believe is best. But my contention is that youngsters don't enjoy that kind of practice, especially limited-participation drills such as batting practice. (They like the hitting part but are rarely as attentive as we'd like while the other kids are batting.) Children prefer games, contests, and competitions. Since it's their practice time, not ours, why not create a practice schedule that excites them? *Making Little League Baseball More Fun for Kids* gives coaches and parents a way to provide skill-work in the guise of games that will keep kids happy and attentive throughout their practice.

Each game is introduced by a brief message or anecdote that relates to the skill being learned. Next, the game is described in detail under the heading "How It's Done." This section provides information about such things as the number of players required, necessary equipment, and a detailed explanation of how to play the game. This is followed by a section titled "Purpose," which explains the specific skills the players will improve. A game, for example, might focus on improving bat control, or baserunning, or throwing accuracy.

Finally, I have included a sidebar along with each game that's designed to entertain as well as teach. Photos and diagrams with captions also accompany the text.

One last suggestion for coaches: Once you arrive at the field, remove the word *work* from your baseball vocabulary. I often hear coaches say things such as, "Tonight we're going to work on cut-offs and relays," or "This afternoon we're going to work on hitting the ball to the opposite field." Since when is playing a game supposed to involve work? Remember that question every time you send those little guys out to their positions and you'll have more fun, too.

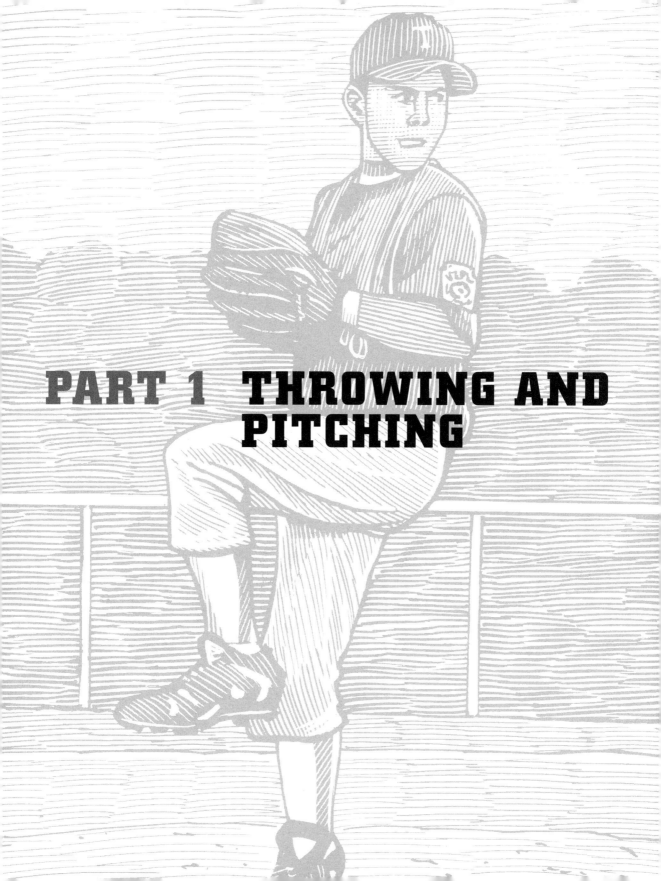

PART 1 THROWING AND PITCHING

BASEBALL IN THE BARREL

When it comes to scouting nonpitchers, baseball's talent evaluators look at five areas of ability: hitting, hitting with power, baserunning, defense, and arm strength. These talents are also known as tools. A player who excels in all five areas is known as a "five-tool" player. I believe we should consider a sixth tool: throwing accuracy. What good is it to have a powerful throwing arm if you can't hit what you're looking at? Poor accuracy means missed cutoffs and overthrows that afford free bases to the opposing team. A strong, *accurate* arm, however, will stop the opponent's running game and reduce them to station-to-station baseball. Here is a great game for improving the skill of precision throwing.

How It's Done

Position all outfielders in a single line in right field. Place a plastic barrel on its side in front of third base and one in front of home plate, with the openings facing right field. Hit fly balls and ground balls to each player and have him attempt to throw the balls into the barrels, first throwing to third, then to home. In each case, the player should pick out a target area where the ball will land before bouncing to the target. Allow each player to make five throws to

After fielding a ground ball or fly ball hit by the coach, the player steps toward third base and tries to throw the ball into the barrel.

each barrel. Points are awarded according to the accuracy of the throws: Any ball landing within three feet of the barrel earns one point; any ball that strikes a barrel without going in earns two points; any ball that goes into a barrel earns three points.

To involve your middle infielders (shortstops and second basemen) in the game, position them in a shallow outfield position with their backs to the infield. Have an outfielder relay the ball to an infielder, then the infielder throws the ball toward the barrel. Move the players to different positions in the outfield to keep the game interesting.

Purpose

The chief benefit of this game is improved throwing accuracy—direction and trajectory—and arm strength. By awarding points for balls thrown into the barrel, you are encouraging the players to

Throwing the ball toward a target on the ground teaches players to aim low. High-sailing overthrows permit runners to advance extra bases.

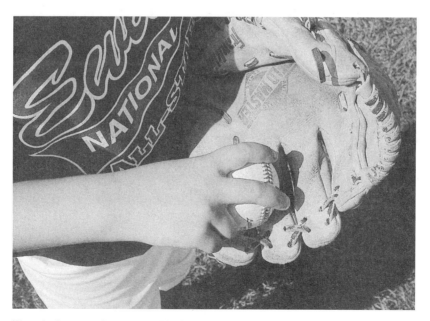

The pitcher needs to keep his fingers on top of the ball. It improves accuracy and creates backspin carry.

focus on precision throwing, and because the easiest way to get the ball into the barrel is by bouncing or rolling it in, the trajectory of the throws will be low—the exact trajectory you want from an outfield throw—so an infielder may cut the ball off, if necessary. Also, consistent throwing from the outfield will improve players' arm strength, making them more effective and confident.

FUNDAMENTAL TIP

Teaching the simple task of throwing the baseball properly is one of the most important things any youth league coach will accomplish. Each player should be treated as though he has never thrown a ball before. The correct way to throw a ball is to grip it across the seams, making sure to keep the fingers on top of the ball, because that's what the pitcher is throwing—the *top of the ball*. Each throw must be directed toward a specific target. The pitcher steps directly toward the target; keeps his lead shoulder closed, using it as a sort of gun sight; and throws the ball overhand, releasing it when his hand is at a 1:00 or 2:00 position, thereby creating maximum backspin and carry. He should throw the ball hard; lower is better than higher.

2

RED, WHITE, AND BLUE PITCHING

The most important element of good pitching is control, the ability to consistently throw the ball over the plate. This is true at any level of the game, including the major leagues. What good is an overpowering fastball if you can't throw it over the plate? Atlanta Braves pitcher Greg Maddux is a great example of a pitcher who has only average velocity (by major-league standards). Maddux is a consistent winner, not because of the speed of his pitches, but because he has such precise control over them. He throws the ball low to the corners of the plate, where hitters have the most trouble making contact. The point is that young pitchers should first learn how to control their pitches, then, as they get bigger and stronger, they can be more concerned about velocity.

Try this fun, challenging game for improving control. The rules of the game encourage pitchers to concentrate on throwing the ball to the corners of the plate, which will get hitters out at any level of competition.

Dividing the plate into three sections forces the pitcher to concentrate on throwing the ball to specific areas of the strike zone, rather than simply throwing it "over the plate."

How It's Done

This is a game for pitchers only. You'll need a portable home plate made of wood or plastic and some household paint. Assuming a right-handed hitter is at bat, paint the inside four inches of the plate white, the outside four inches of the plate blue, and the remaining center part of the plate red. The object of the game is to score as many points as possible by throwing the ball across the corners of the plate. The white and blue sections are worth three points each, and the red section is worth one point. The pitcher may earn two bonus points by "calling his pitch." For example, if the pitcher says he will throw the ball across the blue section and he does, he earns three points for hitting the blue section and two bonus points for calling his pitch. The winner is the pitcher who scores the most points within the amount of pitches designated by the coach, usually 30 to 40. *Catchers should be dressed in full equipment.*

Purpose

Play this game to teach pitchers better control by having them pitch to the corners of the plate, where it is most difficult for batters to put the barrel of the bat on the ball. This is especially important for pitchers who don't have a dominating fastball. The key to their success will be the ability to locate their pitches away from the middle of the plate. The fact that you're keeping score puts some pressure on each pitch, much as the pitchers will feel in a game situation. Also, awarding bonus points for a "called pitch" will encourage the players to throw for a specific corner rather than just throwing the ball for the center of the plate and hoping they catch a corner. By keeping score, pitchers will establish their own personal point record, which they should attempt to better each time they play this game.

The pitcher raises his stride leg until his knee is nearly waist-high and his hips and shoulders are closed to home plate. This is often called the "balance" or "pause position."

FUNDAMENTAL TIP

To consistently throw strikes, a pitcher must have a sound delivery, and the key to a sound delivery is balance. To promote good balance, have your pitcher keep the delivery as simple as possible. Taking the hands over the head or using a huge leg kick may work for big-league pitchers, but they're a bad idea for youngsters. Take your pitcher through these easy steps to build a well-balanced delivery:

1. Stand with the ball in your glove at chest level and your feet shoulder-width apart, with your pivot foot in contact with the rubber (for a right-hander, this is the right foot) and your stride foot slightly behind the rubber.
2. Initiate the delivery by making a "rocker step" with your stride foot, moving it back and to the left a few inches (on a 45-degree angle).
3. Turn your pivot foot 90 degrees and slide it into a position in front of and against the pitching rubber.
4. Raise your stride leg until your knee is near waist-height, with your foot under your knee and your hips and shoulders closed to home plate.
5. Lower your stride leg, removing the ball from your glove about halfway down, and begin to glide toward the plate with your stride leg leading and your upper body trailing. Do not push off the rubber!
6. Bring your stride foot down either square to the plate or slightly closed (1:00 position).
7. Deliver the pitch.
8. Swing your throwing hand and arm down and across your body, finishing somewhere between your knee and foot on your stride-leg side.

3

IN-LINE RELAY THROWING RACE

Many baseball games are won or lost by how well short throws are made and how quickly and securely the ball is transferred from glove to hand. These skills are important for executing such plays as one infielder throwing to another during a double play; the catcher transferring the ball from his glove to his hand so he can make a quick throw to nail a base-stealer; and the outfielder picking the ball up from the base of the fence and throwing to the relay man, who then transfers the ball from his glove to his hand before firing it home to cut off a run. These "little things" make the difference between winning and losing, between an average team and a good team. Every coach should devote time to quick, precise relays and quick, secure ball handling. The In-Line Relay Throwing Race is a great game for developing these skills under the heat of competition.

How It's Done

Divide the team into two squads of equal numbers. Position the squads in two parallel lines approximately 30 feet apart, with each

The key to this game is quick hands and proper foot positioning. It's crucial for each player to deliver an accurate throw to the next man in line and then shift his feet to prepare to receive the next throw.

player at least 20 feet from the teammate in front of and behind him. The player in the front of each line has a baseball. On your signal, he turns and relays the ball to the next player behind him. This continues until the last player in line has received the ball. He then relays it back to the player in front of him. The process continues until the ball is returned to the player at the front of the line. The team that returns the ball to the front of the line first wins the game.

There are a couple of important rules: Errant throws must be retrieved by the player for whom the throw was intended, and every player in the line must catch a throw. No players may be skipped in either direction. You may alter the rules to require as many repetitions along the line as you like. Adjust the lineups until the competition is as close as possible.

On guaranteed doubles, the trail man backs up the cutoff man on throws from the outfield.

Purpose

Winning this game requires precision throwing. Throws must be accurate in direction and elevation, preferably to the teammate's glove side at chest level for easy transferring from glove to hand. Players will learn it is more important to release the ball quickly and accurately than it is to throw it with great velocity. To succeed, they must also be deft at ball handling, moving the ball quickly from glove to hand, while performing under the pressure of competition. Last but not least, the kids will learn the value of teamwork, that their team is only as strong as the weakest link. For example, a strong player paired with a less skilled teammate should recognize the need to adjust his throwing or receiving technique in order for the team to succeed. The selflessness found in good teamwork is essential to winning this game.

14

GAME TIP

It would be a coach's dream if all relay throws were accurate, but they aren't, so we must prepare for the worst. As a player moves into position to receive a relay throw, he should *expect* an errant throw. He needs to get his body into a balanced position, ready to react in any direction. On any ball hit to the fence (a guaranteed double at the least), the relaying infielder—shortstop or second baseman—should be backed up by the other middle infielder, the "trail man." The trail man is positioned behind the relay man and far enough back so he can react to an errant throw, cut it off, and make a play.

4

THE GAME OF 21

Young players can master throwing in two simple steps—and each step can be made into a game. First, they learn the basic movements of the body when throwing. Ingraining this skill builds confidence, prevents bad habits, and prepares young players for the many types of throws that baseball demands. Second, they learn how to master the correct release points that vary between infielders and outfielders. And overall, this simple game puts fun and competition into learning how to throw correctly and accurately.

How It's Done

The first step is to have your players play Phantom Toss, which is throwing an imaginary ball. Start by pairing the players in teams of two and place them about 30 to 40 feet apart. No balls are used—just a glove. Have each player face his partner, then turn 90 degrees to the right (to the left for left-handed players), so his left shoulder now points toward his partner. He now lifts the leg closest to his partner (the left leg for right-handers) and balances on his other leg. All his weight is on the rear, or posting, leg. He flexes the posting leg and rotates his front leg away from his partner. He brings his hands together in front of his chest at shoulder-height.

He should rotate his shoulders until they are perpendicular to an imaginary line between him and his partner. Have each player rotate several times back and forth without dropping his leg. This builds strength in the posting leg and torso muscles and promotes proper balance. This can be difficult for many young players because their leg muscles are not strong enough to support the movement of their upper body. Make a game of this. Set 10 rotations as a goal. Count the number of rotations before each player loses his balance. Be sure to commend those who can reach 10.

Next, each player steps directly toward his partner (90 degrees from the imaginary line he used before) and swings his throwing

The first step in teaching throwing mechanics is to have players play Phantom Toss—throwing an imaginary ball.

A throw that arrives at the receiver's chest is worth one point.

17

hand down, back, and up. His hand should be cocked at the highest point and his elbow level with his shoulder when his lead foot plants on the ground. The player then bends his upper body forward, rotates his upper torso, and squares his hips toward his partner. He brings his throwing hand forward and down and finishes along a path that takes it outside his left knee. This drill-without-a-ball gives players a sense of the full body motion needed to make a powerful throw. It allows them to get the maximum buildup of thrust with the most economical body motion.

Now, add the baseballs. Give each pair of players a ball and have them practice the same movement. The targets are an imaginary rectangle formed at the top and bottom by the partner's shoulder and waist, and an imaginary rectangle around by the partner's head. If a throw arrives within the chest rectangle, score a point. If it comes within the head boundaries, score two points. The first player to get 21 points wins the game. Winners and losers pair off until there is a winner in each bracket. In the play-off rounds, reduce the winning point total to 11 to speed up the competition and promote concentration.

In subsequent practices, increase the distance between players by increments of five feet until they are throwing 70 to 75 feet.

Purpose

Here you are teaching proper throwing mechanics, which include bending forward with the back and leg muscles, rotating with the torso muscles, and getting the hand and elbow up to shoulder level before snapping the wrist as the ball passes by the ear upon release of the ball. You are also teaching players how to throw without putting unnecessary strain or stress on the joints, muscles, tendons, and ligaments in their shoulders, arms, and elbows, which are the most vulnerable. By promoting the use of the big muscles of the back, torso, and legs, you are minimizing the risk of injury to the upper limbs.

By incorporating the targets—head and shoulder-to-waist areas—you are teaching accuracy. The above-the-waist targets are the most useful in this game because you are acclimating the player to delivering the ball at the level that is most practicable for infielders and outfielders when transferring the ball from the glove to throwing hand and then into a throwing motion. However, you can also use this game with pitchers. Simply have your catcher squat, and use for a target the triangle formed by the top of the catcher's head and the tips of his shoulders.

FUNDAMENTAL TIP

After your players have mastered this drill, you can adapt it for various positions. This means having the infielders and catcher employing an abbreviated throwing motion that releases the ball at 2:00 (imagine the face of a clock and bring the throwing hand to approximately 2:00 as it swings forward). Outfielders make the throw from a more overhead position, at approximately 1:00. They should not raise the arm any higher (to 12:00)—this is incorrect and risks injury. The infielders and catchers initiate their throws with a crow hop, a shorter step, and an abbreviated bend and rotation. This gets the ball out of the glove and up into the throwing position quicker. It makes for a short, powerful throw. Major-league infielder Roberto Alomar exhibits the short, quick motion that players should try to emulate.

Outfielders take a longer stride toward the target and release closer to 1:00. A good example of the desired throwing action for outfielders is that of major-league outfielder Vladimir Guerrero. He has a terrifically accurate and powerful throwing arm and classic technique.

Now the players are training themselves for the throws they will have to make under game conditions.

5

PLAYING CATCH
MARATHON

eams throw in practice sessions to get their arms loose, to build arm strength, and to simulate plays from their respective positions. It's rare, however, to see players throw for the purpose of developing accuracy. Throwing accuracy is essential to becoming an all-around efficient defensive player. Players with strong throwing arms are valuable only if they can throw the ball on target.

Playing catch can become boring for kids, but attach competition to it and it becomes their favorite exercise. Playing Catch Marathon is a game that allows them to work on proper throwing mechanics while stoking their competitive fire.

How It's Done

Have all your players pair off. Each pair should stand approximately 35 to 40 feet apart. At your call, players simply step and throw the ball back and forth to each other. Each pair survives in the game as long as the ball never touches the ground. If the ball is thrown short, flies past the receiver, or is dropped by the receiver, the pair is eliminated. Make sure players use proper form when throwing the ball. Repeating incorrect movements will ingrain poor mechanics.

Using the across-the-seams grip, the player takes the ball out of the glove and moves his hand back and up, until his elbow is approximately at shoulder-height. This backswing is relatively short, nothing more than a quick loop back and up. He positions his hand so the upper and lower parts of his arm form a right angle at his elbow. At the same time, he steps toward his target with his left foot (if he's a right-handed thrower) and points his glove arm toward the target, while rotating his shoulders and hips until they are in a direct line with his target. He pushes his weight back on the ball-side foot.

As his arm accelerates into the throw, he pivots on the ball of his back foot and shifts his weight from his back foot to his front. When he releases the ball, he should feel it rotate off his fingertips. At the same time, he pulls his lead arm into his chest, near his heart, as he shifts his weight forward.

Remind players to finish the throw by following through. The thrower shouldn't stop his arm after the ball has left his hand. He needs to fully extend his arm toward his target. The sign of a good follow-through is that the throwing hand finishes across the thrower's body outside of the opposite leg, between the knee and shin.

Players continue throwing back and forth until the ball touches the ground. The ball must be thrown crisply on a straight line. Any lobs or soft throws and the pair is immediately disqualified.

To make the game more difficult, back the players up a few steps and have them throw from 50 to 60 feet. If it's just two players who want to work alone on their throwing accuracy, have them keep count of their throws and record the highest number.

Players throw the ball back and forth with a partner. Whichever pair continues the longest without an errant throw wins the game.

Purpose

By facing the possibility of elimination with each throw, players will feel pressure to throw the ball accurately. This simulates game-like conditions. They're forced to focus and execute on every throw and catch.

Although this game may seem monotonous at times, players are building arm strength and developing proper throwing mechanics in the process. The only way to ingrain the correct movements in a player's brain and body is to repeat an action over and over again; Playing Catch Marathon accomplishes this.

The game forces players to work on receiving the ball as well. If they lose their concentration, they risk dropping or missing the ball. Players will build confidence and become more sure-handed when catching the ball.

24

COACHING TIP

Building arm strength lets a player throw the ball harder, farther, and for a longer period of time (building endurance). There is only one way to increase arm strength, and that is throwing—period. Let it be said one more time: To increase arm strength, a player must throw regularly.

Many coaches and parents are under the impression that constant rest allows an arm to stay fresh. This is a grave error in judgment. You've got to throw the baseball regularly to increase velocity and longevity. Nursing the arm and treating it like a precious antique will diminish performance and contribute to the possibility of injury. If a player feels a little soreness, that's okay. In fact, it's expected. It's not a reason to shut a player down and tell him he can't throw for an extended period of time.

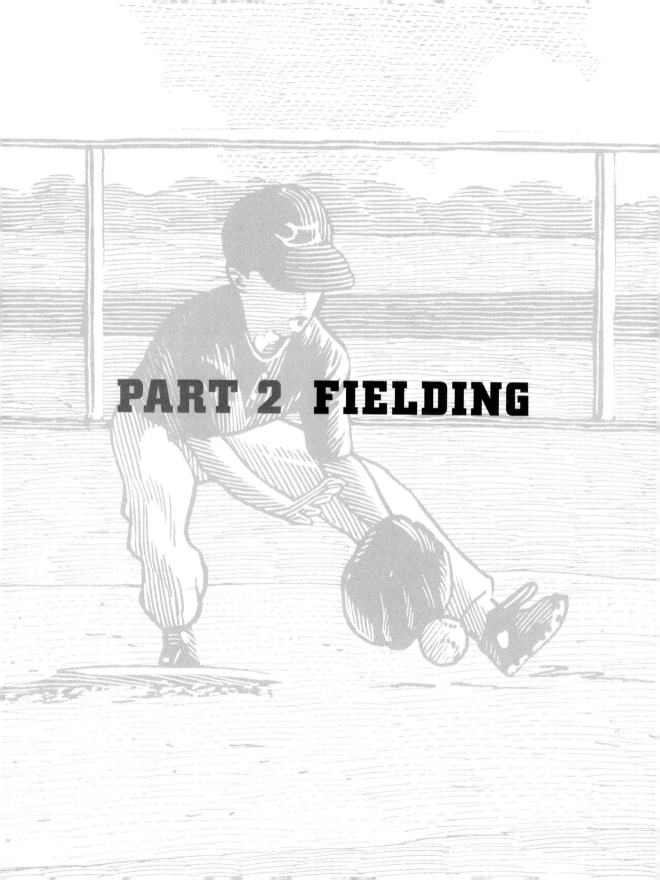

PART 2 FIELDING

6

WIDE RECEIVER

One of the toughest things for young players to learn—and for coaches to teach—is how to catch fly balls while running. Players cannot rely on getting a steady diet of fly balls in game situations, and the coach faces the difficult task of hitting fly balls that are either too easy or too hard to catch. I believe the best way to teach this skill is to borrow a concept from football. I have found the Wide Receiver game is the best way to teach and learn the art of catching a ball on the run and turning those long fly balls into outs instead of hits.

How It's Done

Position all the players single file at the right field line, facing center field. Stand about five feet away from the line with a ball in your hand and a bucket of balls at your feet. At your command, the first player in line sprints toward center field, as though he were a wide receiver running for a "pass" from you, the "quarterback." Throw passes to each player. After catching or retrieving his pass, the player then circles behind you, places the ball in the bucket, and returns to the end of the line. Alternate your throws, tossing some

The player sprints toward center field, glancing back every few steps to find the ball. The ball is thrown over his left shoulder, forcing him to make a tough catch on the run.

long, some short, some high, some low, some over the left shoulder, and some over the right. Each player should receive 10 to 12 passes.

Purpose

This game yields several benefits. First, it helps players learn how to catch the ball on the run. Second, players can condition their bodies without the monotony of standard running drills. Third, it is much easier to expose players to a wide variety of ball flights with this drill than it is with a fungo bat. Fourth, it's fun, because the kids love to compete with one another to run the most creative patterns and make the most spectacular catches. And fifth, you can teach the valuable "neck whip" technique, in which a player running with his back to the infield learns to change direction quickly and efficiently by merely whipping his neck from one side to the other. Anyone who has seen a youngster corkscrew himself into the ground while pursuing a fly ball will appreciate the value of this drill.

PRACTICE TIP

One of the traits shared by all good outfielders is their ability to get a *jump* on the ball. That is, they anticipate the ball being hit, and their first step is quick and on the correct angle to intercept it. Some baseball people believe that a good jump is an instinctive move that can't be learned. I disagree. There are a few simple things a player must do to get a better jump on a batted ball.

First, he must believe that the ball will be put into play on every pitch. This requires great discipline. Second, he must watch the pitched ball all the way into the hitting zone. He will soon realize that pitches toward the outside part of the hitting zone are likely to be hit to the opposite field, and that pitches in the middle and inside parts of the zone are most often hit to the pull side of the field. By watching the flight of the pitch, the player will learn to anticipate where the ball will be hit. Last but not least, he must be physically prepared to move for the ball. The key element here is to have his feet in motion as the ball reaches the hitting zone. Happy feet are better than flat feet.

7

STAR GROUNDERS

Every coach would agree that it's important for infielders to field ground balls as often as possible, taking 30 to 40 grounders during every practice session. The problem for coaches, though, is finding enough time to ensure that every infielder gets enough ground balls to keep improving. For younger players, the best way around this time constraint is for players to supply ground balls to one another. They can do this by playing a game I call Star Grounders.

How It's Done

Divide your players into groups of five. (Although this is primarily a game for infielders, it will benefit other players, too.) Position each group such that each player represents one point on a star. No player should be closer than 40 feet from another, and each group gets a ball. The game starts when the player with the ball rolls a grounder to the player two positions to his left. That player then rolls a grounder to the player two positions to his left, and so on. After each player has fielded six or eight balls, change the direction of the game by rolling grounders to the player two positions to the right. Make the game more interesting by instructing players to vary the types of grounders: some fast, some slow, some directly at their teammate, some slightly to his left or right. Have them use a sidearm technique to get the ball rolling as quickly as possible. Instruct the players to track their progress by counting the number of balls they field cleanly each time they play the game.

Purpose

This is the ideal game for exposing players to the maximum number of ground balls in the shortest period of time (and allowing the coach more time for working on other skills during practice). Remember, most kids are introduced to the game by playing catch; they spend most of their time catching balls thrown in the air. The rest of their time is usually spent learning how to hit. They spend very little time fielding ground balls. Don't assume they have any formal training or have spent much practice time on this.

Learning to field ground balls consistently is not a difficult task, yet misplayed grounders account for the vast majority of errors in

Each player should roll the ball crisply to his teammates. When fielding grounders, players need to remember to reach out for the ball with the glove and keep their rear end down.

youth baseball. It is very discouraging when the pitcher throws a strike that produces a ground ball, only to have the batter reach base because the ball was "booted." Fielding ground balls must become a routine task for all players if you are to have a winning team. Keep the other team to three outs per inning, and you will usually have a chance to win the game. Give them more than three outs, and you're in trouble. By using the Star Grounders game during every practice, more ground balls will become outs, and your team will spend more time where it wants to be—at bat!

COACHING TIP

Hitting and pitching are certainly the most glamorous elements of baseball. They receive far more attention than fielding—too much more attention. To be a winning coach, you must change the perception among your players that fielding is less important than hitting or pitching. One way to do this is to challenge the notion that the team at bat is the offense, and that scoring runs is more important than recording outs.

I explain to my players that the team in the field is really the offense. That's partly because we have the ball and are therefore able to dictate the pace of the game, and also because we are taking away the other team's outs. We are attacking, and that's what an offense does.

Remember, in a six-inning game, each team is given 18 outs to play with, and excepting extra innings, there is nothing they can do to get more. If you are efficient at taking away the other team's outs—more efficient than they are at taking away yours—you have an excellent chance of winning the game. By fielding balls cleanly and making accurate throws, you strip your opponents of their outs and their ability to score.

33

8

THE GOALIE GAME

Wouldn't it be great if your pitcher had such precise control that the catcher never had to block a pitch in the dirt? And wouldn't it be nice if your infielders threw the ball so accurately that your first baseman never had to scoop a ball out of the dirt? But errant pitches and throws happen at every level of baseball, even in the major leagues. How these plays are handled represents the difference between out and safe; a run scoring or not scoring; an inning ending or continuing; and, ultimately, winning and losing. It makes sense to devote practice time to something that may have such a dramatic effect on the game's outcome. Here's a fun game that will make your catchers and first basemen more proficient at handling those balls in the dirt.

How It's Done

This game is for catchers and first basemen. Let's deal with the catchers first. You will need a net similar in configuration to those used for street hockey. Four feet wide by four feet high would be ideal, although something four feet wide will suffice. Have the catcher put on *all his protective equipment* and assume his position behind the plate, with the net squarely behind him and about two feet back. Throw balls to the catcher, alternating between

To properly block a ball in the dirt, the catcher drops to his knees and leans forward with his upper body to cradle the ball. It's important for him to keep his head down and curl his shoulders inward to keep the ball in front of him.

If you don't have access to a hockey goal, place two cones approximately four feet apart. The catcher's job is not to let the ball pass between the cones!

pitches in the air and in the dirt. (You throw pitches in the air—hopefully some strikes—so he can't immediately drop into the blocking position. His first responsibility is to catch the ball in the air. Don't allow him to cheat.) Much like a hockey goalie, the catcher's job is to keep the ball out of the net. Work on his technique for getting his body in front of balls in the dirt, sliding side to side, and making sure that he uses his glove to block the hole between his legs. Count the number of "goals" the catcher allows so you can monitor his progress throughout the season.

The process is much the same for the first baseman, although you can use a larger net if one is available. (*It may be wise to have the first baseman wear protective catcher's gear the first few times you play this game.*) Starting at a distance of 30 feet, throw balls to the first baseman, alternating between accurate throws and throws in the dirt. Throw some right at him, some to his left, and some to his right. You may increase the distance according to his age and ability. Work on the player's technique, emphasizing that his first responsibility is to keep the ball from getting past him, even if he must break contact with the bag to do so. Award bonus points if he scoops the ball cleanly while maintaining contact with the bag. Again, count the number of "goals" allowed and keep a record throughout the season.

Purpose

Dealing smartly with pitches and throws in the dirt will keep the opponent from getting extra outs, extra bases, and extra runs. For example, stopping a runner from advancing from first to second base on a pitch in the dirt keeps the force play in order, the double play in order, and the runner from scoring on a single—or maybe even a double. One "little" play by the catcher changes the whole complexion of the inning.

You'll also notice that the pitchers and infielders will become more relaxed and confident as they realize that their every pitch or throw doesn't have to be perfect. Trust among teammates is a wonderful thing.

FUNDAMENTAL TIP

Remind players: You don't want to *catch* the pitch in the dirt; you want to *block* it with your body. This is especially true of pitches off the sides of the plate. Whenever possible, avoid reaching for these pitches. This requires more hand-to-eye coordination and dexterity than you may have. The correct method is to drop and slide to the side, moving to center your body behind the ball. Once you've blocked the ball, it is just a matter of finding it, grabbing it, and checking the position of the runner.

9

KNOCKOUT

A good fielder is proud of his defensive skills, and in crucial situations, he wants the ball to be hit to him. There's a lot of pressure when the game is on the line, when you know that one bobble or poor throw will cause your team to lose. It's not easy to replicate this high-pressure situation in practice, but you can come close if you play a game of Knockout.

How It's Done

Although this is primarily a game for infielders, anyone can play. Put the first baseman in his normal position and have everyone else line up single file on the outfield grass behind the shortstop position. One by one, the players step forward and assume the shortstop position. You begin the game by hitting a ground ball, which the player must field cleanly—no fumbling—then make an accurate throw to first. Players who complete the play return to the line. Those who don't are eliminated from the game.

You may adjust the rules by placing the players at some position other than shortstop, or you may decide to eliminate players only after a second mistake. To increase the pace—and the pressure— of the game, move the players to a position no more than 30 to 40

To stay in the game, each player has to field the ball cleanly and make an accurate throw to first base. Tell participants to stay relaxed and focused to give themselves the best chance of surviving later rounds.

feet from where you're standing. To take the game to a more advanced level, use eliminated players as base runners. The runner starts at home plate and leaves for first as soon as your bat makes contact with the ball. If the fielder fails to get the ball to first in time, he is eliminated from the game.

Purpose

The game promotes good fielding form and accurate throwing under the pressure of competition. Players must focus intently on both tasks: catching the ground ball, then making a good throw to first base. Any lapse in concentration will result in elimination from the game. This is a great game for measuring the progress of your fielders. If a player can survive more than a dozen rounds of Knockout competition, where no mistakes are allowed, he should be able to handle difficult game situations.

A bobbled ball or errant throw eliminates the player (shown walking) from the game.

TRY THIS

Another variation of Knockout is called Machine Gun. In this game, the players must each field five ground balls in rapid-fire succession. (After every ground ball, the player must make an accurate throw to a designated base.) As soon as the player has released the ball, you hit another grounder to him. This game requires total concentration, because the ground balls are coming fast and furious. The game is a good conditioning tool, too. After three or four rounds of Machine Gun, there will be tongues, including the coach's, hanging out all over the field.

10

OUTFIELDER-INFIELDERS RELAY

Thereare few things in baseball more exciting than watching an outfielder and infielders perfectly execute a relay play to cut down a runner at the plate. This requires absolute precision by the defense: The outfielder must pick up the ball cleanly and make a strong, accurate throw to the infielder; the infielder must catch the ball, quickly transfer it to his throwing hand, and fire it to the catcher. These plays often decide the outcome of a game, so it's important to practice them frequently. You can introduce an element of fun and competition into this practice by playing the Outfielder-Infielders Relay race.

How It's Done

Create as many three-man teams as you can, each consisting of one outfielder and two middle infielders. (You may allow your corner infielders to participate as middle infielders.) Have the players start in their normal positions. Place a ball against the outfield fence. At the sound of your whistle, the outfielder sprints from his position to retrieve the ball. The middle infielder closest to the ball—the

At the sound of the whistle, the outfielders race to gather the ball at the fence.

lead infielder—moves toward the outfielder, out onto the grass. The other middle infielder—the *trail infielder*—moves in about 15 to 20 feet behind the other infielder, on a direct line between the outfielder and home plate. (If the ball is in left center field, the shortstop is the lead and the second baseman is the trail. If the ball is in right center field, the second baseman is the lead and the shortstop is the trail.) The outfielder picks up the ball with his throwing hand and throws it to the lead infielder, who then relays the ball to home plate. The trail infielder is in position in case the relay throw from the outfielder sails over, around, or through the lead infielder. In that case, the trail catches the ball and relays it to the catcher. Record each team's time, from whistle to the ball's arrival at the plate, with a stopwatch. The team that executes the relay play in the fastest time—without any errant throws—is the winner. Each team gets a minimum of four tries.

Purpose

This game affords players an opportunity to practice defensive teamwork, an absolute essential for winning ball games. You will demonstrate that on defense the players are dependent on one another. A breakdown by one player means a breakdown by the entire team.

On an individual level, players will be practicing precision throwing, quick transferring of the ball from glove to throwing hand, and functioning under pressure. Another benefit of this game is that they will learn that solid defense creates opportunities for the team to turn a negative (a base hit by the opposition) into a positive (an out).

To simulate the pressure of a game, add a base runner to the game and let him try to score.

GAME TIP

Good communication, both visual and verbal, is essential for successfully executing a relay play. As he reaches his position on the outfield grass, the lead infielder should place his hands above his head to provide a target for the outfielder to throw to. At the same time, he should yell instructions, like "Hit me. Hit me." If the trail infielder sees an errant throw from the outfielder, one that won't be easy for the lead infielder to catch, he should call out, "Let it go. I've got it." Finally, the catcher, the eyes of the defense, must tell the relay man where to throw the ball, yelling out a number designation for a base: "Four, four," or "Three, three." Good communication lessens the chance of the ball being thrown to the wrong base—a cardinal sin in baseball.

11

THE CATCHER'S GLOVE GAME

The comment "He's got good hands" is often used to describe a slick-moving infielder. What does the term *good hands* mean? It doesn't mean that one player was born with hands better-suited for fielding ground balls than another player. It means that through repetitive practice the infielder has learned how to make his hands work efficiently, sometimes together, sometimes alone. An infielder with good hands has mastered fundamental techniques, developed quick reflexes, and become confident in his abilities. There are many teaching methods for improving an infielder's defensive skills. I believe the first thing he must learn is how to make his hands work together. A great way to work on this skill is to have your infielders practice fielding ground balls with a catcher's glove.

How It's Done

During infield practice, have the players take turns wearing a catcher's glove. Each player must field 20 ground balls while wearing that glove. Hit balls directly to the infielder, to his left, and to

Fielding the ball with a catcher's glove forces players to use their throwing hand to secure the ball in the pocket.

his right. Hit slow rollers that he must charge, field, and throw to first. Keep track of each player's score: one point for each ball fielded cleanly and zero points for any error. Tracking their scores over the course of the season will help you to assess their rate of improvement.

Purpose

Since it is much harder to field ground balls with a catcher's glove, this drill will help players build good fundamental skills, such as using their throwing hand to gather the ball into the glove. Also, the pocket of the catcher's glove is much smaller than that of an ordinary infielder's glove, so the player's use of the glove hand must be very precise in order to catch the ball in the pocket. The catcher's glove is unwieldy, too—very bulky and heavy—so the infielder must get into excellent fielding position to catch the ball. Failure to position his body correctly will result in the player's having to reach for the ball; this is very difficult to do with a large, cumbersome catcher's glove. This game can be especially helpful for a better player, who can often get by on talent alone and eschew proper fielding techniques.

TRY THIS

If your budget can stand it, buy a "glove" specially designed for teaching infielders to use both hands when fielding a ground ball. This training tool looks more like a leather Ping-Pong paddle than a baseball glove; it's absolutely flat, with no pocket. You put the paddle on your hand and field ground balls. Because there is no pocket, the only way to catch the ball is to use your throwing hand to secure the ball against the paddle. I have used this glove for training purposes, and I recommend it. It is available through most baseball merchandise catalogs.

12

POP-FLY PRIORITIES

Short fly balls into the shallow outfield area are too often a nightmare for coaches and players. What should be a sure out turns into a hit, or worse yet, an injury. Trouble usually arrives in the form of miscommunication between the infielders and out-fielders. On some occasions, all the fielders back off and allow the ball to fall safely to the ground. Other times, everyone pursues the ball and the result is a dangerous collision. All of this is avoidable, because there is a very easy and safe way to practice this play. All you need is a tennis racket and tennis ball.

How It's Done

Send all of your fielders, except the pitcher and catcher, out to their positions. You're going to stand near the pitcher's mound and serve pop-fly tennis balls into the shallow outfield, covering the area from foul line to foul line. Before you start, however, you must train your players on the proper way to communicate with one another.

First, the outfielders always have priority, because it is easier to come in on a ball than go back on one. The outfielders must be instructed to call for and catch any ball they can reach. They must call for the ball with a uniform verbal sign: "I got it. I got it." Tell

It's much easier to simulate pop flies by hitting tennis balls with a racquet. The wind also has a greater effect on tennis balls, which teaches kids to stay with the ball throughout its descent.

52

them to yell, to scream if they have to. Once the outfielder makes the call, all the other players who were pursuing the ball should peel away while yelling, "Take it. Take it." Make sure each player understands that he should pursue each pop fly aggressively with the intention of catching it, until another player calls for the ball. This is especially true for infielders. Even though outfielders have priority, they may not be able to reach every pop fly, so it's important for the infielders to pursue the ball as well. If an outfielder and infielder call for the ball simultaneously, *the outfielder always has priority*. If two outfielders simultaneously call for the ball, *the center fielder always has priority*. The right or left fielder must back away and yell, "Take it. Take it." If two infielders call for the ball at the same time, the second baseman has priority over the first baseman—he usually has a better angle to the ball—and the shortstop has priority over the third baseman for the same reason. If the shortstop and second baseman both call it, the shortstop has priority, because the ball is most likely to his glove side.

You can make a game of Pop-Fly Priorities by having the left side of the defense compete against the right side. (The center fielder plays for both teams.) Whichever team allows the fewest pop flies to reach the ground wins the game.

Purpose

First and foremost, this drill helps players learn how to avoid colliding with one another. Use it for that, if for no other reason. Second, you want to train your players to become comfortable and

Communication between players is very important when chasing a pop fly destined to land in a neutral area.

aggressive when pursuing those in-between pop flies that often fall safely to the ground. The good communication skills they learn will increase their confidence, allowing them to take advantage of every opportunity to get an easy out.

The game also helps them learn their "range," that is, how far they can travel to catch the ball. The middle infielders, in particular, will get better at taking the proper angles to the ball. Watch how quickly the shortstop and second baseman learn to take the correct path to short pop flies down the foul lines. Soon they'll be catching pop flies in foul territory!

TRY THIS

The tennis racket and ball may also be used to teach pop-fly priorities within the infield. The pitchers and catchers can participate in this drill, too. Also, it's a great way to train your catcher to catch pop flies. (All coaches know how difficult it is to hit pop flies to the catcher with a bat and ball!) Just remember to tell the catcher that the one thing you can't simulate with the tennis ball is backspin. The baseball will come off the bat with backspin, which makes the ball spin back toward the infield. The tennis ball won't do that, but the catcher will still learn how to find the ball, jettison his mask, and position himself for the catch.

13

AROUND THE HORN

Many of the most important throws in a baseball game are made from one base to another: from second to first on a double play attempt; from home to second (or third) in an attempt to nail a base-stealer; from first to home on the 1-2-3 double play; and from any base to home in an attempt to prevent a runner from scoring. It makes sense, then, that we should devote ample practice time to throwing the ball from base to base. One of the best ways to do this is to throw the ball "around the horn," which means it starts at home plate and is thrown either clockwise or counterclockwise around the bases. You can easily turn this seemingly mundane exercise into a fun game that kids will enjoy.

How It's Done

This is a game for infielders and catchers. Divide the players into teams of four, with one fielder at each base and a catcher at home plate. (If necessary, use pitchers or outfielders to make at least two complete teams.) Beginning with the catcher, the players must throw the ball clockwise (home to third to second to first to home) around the horn, base by base, without the ball touching the ground. After four trips around the horn, the direction is reversed, so the ball is travelling in a counterclockwise direction. The direction is reversed every four trips thereafter. Teams are awarded one point for each base the ball travels without touching the ground. The team that accumulates the most points wins the game.

You may also involve noninfielders in the game by having them back up the bases. If an outfielder is able to field an errant throw and accurately relay the ball to the next base, the team gets credit for that base.

Purpose

This game helps the players to practice many vital defensive skills: catching; throwing; and quick, efficient transferring of the ball from glove to hand. As a bonus, they learn to do these things under competitive conditions. They also learn the correct velocity and trajectory for accurately throwing the ball from one base to another. And just as important, they learn to function as a team.

The catcher initiates the game by throwing the ball to the third baseman.

An accurate throw to home scores a team another point in this practice contest. That same throw during a game may keep the opposition from notching up another run on the scoreboard.

PRACTICE TIP

After your infielders and catchers have loosened their arms at the beginning of practice, have them play a game of catch in which they practice transferring the ball quickly from glove to hand, followed by a strong, accurate throw to their partner. The catchers should treat every throw as though they were attempting to catch a base-stealer. Pay close attention to their footwork and ball exchange, and make sure their hands don't drop below chest-level as they move into throwing position. This practice regimen will prepare them for playing Around the Horn.

14

TENNIS LOBS BEHIND HOME PLATE

When a team is in the field, outs are precious. You must take advantage of any opportunity to record one; if you don't, you can bet it will come back to haunt you later. Outs keep the game moving for the pitcher, and the quicker they're accounted for, the fewer pitches he's forced to throw.

If the pitcher throws a pitch good enough to induce the batter to hit a foul pop, the catcher can't fumble the opportunity to secure the out. A pop-up behind home plate can be a difficult play for a catcher. He has to turn his back to the infield, find the ball in the air, race into position without tripping, toss his catcher's mask aside, and set up where the ball will land. This is easier said than done. The ball will have severe backspin and carry back toward the infield. Tennis Lobs Behind Home Plate is a great drill to improve a catcher's proficiency at catching foul pop-ups.

How It's Done

Have the catcher squat behind home plate. Stand a few feet behind him with a tennis racquet and tennis ball. Toss the ball to yourself and hit a high pop-up straight up in the air. (Try to apply the same spin to the ball that a foul pop would have in a game. In this case, cut under the ball so it lifts with spin that rotates clockwise.)

As you hit the ball, yell, "Ball!" The catcher should jump out of his squat, take off his mask, and turn to find the ball. Once he locates the ball, he should run underneath it and toss his mask. The catcher should not toss his helmet and mask before finding the ball. Doing so creates another obstacle on the ground he could potentially trip over.

After the catcher is under the ball, he should take two steps backward toward the infield to compensate for the backspin on the ball during its descent. The two steps back put him in perfect position.

Continue the drill. At times, hit balls toward the third baseline and first baseline. These are tougher to catch but simulate situa-

Hitting foul pop-ups behind home plate is no easy task. To improve your rate of proficiency, use tennis balls and a racquet when hitting balls to the catcher.

After finding the ball, the catcher tosses his helmet and mask, turns his back to the infield, and makes the catch.

tions that happen in a game. Don't stop the drill until the catcher has caught 10 consecutive balls.

Purpose

The most critical point in fielding a catcher pop-up is finding the ball. If you find it first, at least you have a shot at catching it. Younger players panic and attempt to run to a spot before locating the ball in the air. This drill stresses the importance of finding the ball immediately after it's been hit.

Through trial and error, players will eventually recognize the flight pattern of pop-ups behind home plate. Early on, they'll completely miss balls or fall backward trying to catch them. This is because they haven't yet learned to factor in the backspin. In trying to catch ball after ball, they'll come to understand that the ball carries back toward the infield every time.

GAME TIP

When a ball is popped up behind home plate, it's the catcher's ball. He is not only the closest, but he is also the player who is trained to catch them. This does not mean, however, that the cornermen (third baseman and first baseman) should stay put at their positions. Their job is to back up the catcher when the ball is hit to their respective side of the field. Even major-league players practice this just in case a mishap occurs. Two former major leaguers who would certainly agree are Bob Boone and Pete Rose.

During Game 6 of the 1980 World Series, the Phillies were leading the Royals 4–1 in the bottom of the ninth inning. Phillies reliever Tug McGraw was looking to close out the game for their first world championship. McGraw ran into trouble as he issued a walk and surrendered two singles to load the bases with one out.

Royals second baseman Frank White stepped up to the plate and hit a foul pop-up toward the first base dugout. Phillies catcher Bob Boone ran over to make the catch. As Boone squeezed his glove to record the out, the ball popped out. Fortunately for the Phils, first baseman Pete Rose was standing alongside Boone to back him up. Rose snared the ball before it hit the ground for the second out.

McGraw struck out Willie Wilson to end the game and set off a wild celebration in Philadelphia. If Rose hadn't backed up his catcher on the play, who knows what might have happened? The Phillies might still be seeking their first world championship.

PART 3 HITTING

15

HIT 'EM WHERE
THEY AIN'T

Whenever you watch a major-league game, notice how the defensive players adjust their position, forward and back, left and right, according to who the batter is. They move in part because most hitters have tendencies at the plate, such as a pull hitter who uses only one part of the field. These hitters are easier to pitch to and defend against than hitters who use the whole field by demonstrating bat control.

Since aluminum bats with their larger sweet spots and lighter weights are now used throughout youth baseball, bat control has become a lost art, with most hitters making the same swing at every pitch—a swing designed to pull the ball. That's a mistake. You may hit for more power, but you'll strike out a lot more, too. Contrast that with a hitter such as New York Mets all-star second baseman Edgardo Alfonzo, a real magician with the bat, who hits the ball for average and with power to all fields. Bat control can and should be taught and learned. Here is an easy and fun game that will help your players learn the value of good bat control.

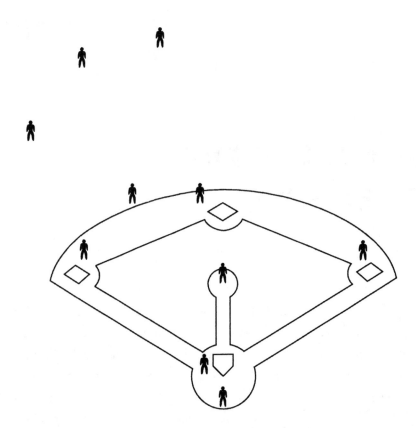

With a right-handed hitter batting, move all your fielders except the first baseman to the left side of the field. This teaches the batter to concentrate on hitting to the opposite field.

How It's Done

Align your fielders in a special "shift" defense. Against a right-handed hitter, all fielders—except the first baseman—move toward the left side of the field, so there is only one remaining fielder to the right side of second base. (The first baseman must stay at first base, with his foot in contact with the bag at all times.) Against a left-handed batter, all fielders move to the right side of second base. The remaining players form the offensive team. Have the pitcher deliver the ball at batting-practice speed, or pitch the game yourself. Encourage every hitter to hit the ball to the opposite field. Each player bats until he makes an out; when that happens, he changes places with one of the fielders. The game continues until every player has batted a minimum of three times.

Purpose

By playing this game, you are teaching your players the forgotten art of bat control. To hit the ball to the opposite field, the batter must wait on the pitch, letting it get deeper into the strike zone. This has several benefits: First, it allows the batter more time to watch the pitch and determine whether it is good to hit. Second, it helps to eliminate the batting flaw of "stepping into the bucket," or opening the hips prematurely and directing the stride foot away from the pitch. (You can't step into the bucket and consistently hit the ball to the opposite field.) And third, using the entire field will

Choking up an inch or two greatly improves bat control.

make the hitter more dangerous, because he will be able to handle any pitch location, and the defense won't be able to make any assumptions about where the ball will be hit.

In this game, hitting the ball to the opposite field, which is unoccupied, will allow the batter to get lots of bases—and lots of at bats. Pulling the ball, however, will almost always result in an out, and a long wait for his next turn. Keep score to see who is good at hitting the ball "where they ain't," as legendary player Wee Willie Keeler used to say. Keeping score will also allow you to measure each batter's progress over the course of the season.

PRACTICE TIP

Pulling every pitch in batting practice is easy, because the pitcher is throwing the ball more slowly than in game conditions. This will give the batter a false sense of security. He won't see those kinds of pitches during a real game, so pulling everything becomes a much harder chore, and one that will inevitably lead to all sorts of hitting flaws. The best way to ensure that batting practice is productive is to make hitting the ball to the opposite field a mandatory part of every session. I recommend that each player begin by laying down two sacrifice bunts, then hitting two balls to the opposite field. This is a good way to start, because both bunting and opposite-field hitting allow the batter to see the ball longer before committing; it gets him into the flow of things. Next, the batter should take seven to eight swings, hitting the ball where it's pitched. Finally, have him finish up with two more hits to the opposite field. Seeing the ball longer and making contact with it deeper in the hitting zone will prepare your batters for game conditions, when the pitches are travelling at a higher speed.

16

HIT THE L-SCREEN

Consistently hitting a baseball back through the middle, past the pitcher and into center field, is not an easy thing to do. But trying to do it is a *good* thing. Hitting the ball this way requires good hitting mechanics, such as a square stride (right back at the pitcher); a short, compact swing, keeping your hands inside the path of the pitch; and seeing the pitch a little longer than you do when you pull the ball.

Also, when a batter does hit the ball back through the middle, he benefits from the pitcher being the nearest fielder. That is, the pitcher doesn't have much time to react to the hit, so the ball often scoots into center field for a hit. And there's another bonus to trying to hit the ball back through the middle: If the batter is a little early or a little late with the bat, the result is often a line drive into an outfield gap. So, grab your L-screen and play a game that will help your players learn how to send the ball back through the middle. Then watch the base hits pile up.

How It's Done

Place an L-screen 15 feet in front of home plate and on a direct line between the plate and the pitching rubber. Set up a batting tee on

With a coach throwing from a shortened distance, the batter attempts to hit each ball back into the screen.

home plate. Direct each batter to hit the ball directly into the L-screen. Make this drill into a contest by declaring that the winner will be the batter who hits five balls into the screen—both line drives and ground balls count—in the fewest number of attempts. Next, move the L-screen back to a distance of 30 feet and pitch balls to the batter. The rules of the contest remain the same. (The distance between the L-screen and the batter may be adjusted according to the age and ability of your players.)

Purpose

Again, you are teaching the lost art of bat control by forcing each batter to manipulate his hands and try to hit the ball to a very precise location. Also, to consistently hit the ball back through the middle, the batter will be forced to stride square, or straight back at the pitcher, the most balanced position a hitter can achieve. Good balance is perhaps the most important ingredient of good hitting form. In the throwing part of the game, the batter must allow the ball to get to a position over the plate, where he has the most power, rather than way out in front of the plate where he will often contact the ball in an unbalanced and weakened position. This, too, helps cure hitting flaws such as striding open or closed, or allowing the barrel of the bat to dip, which most often produces fly balls to the opposite field. Any drill that promotes line drives and ground balls will make your hitters more successful. And more success means more fun.

Whether the pitch is an inside strike, outside strike, or straight down the middle, the hitter *always* strides directly back toward the pitcher.

PRACTICE TIP

Once your players have mastered the L-screen hitting game, go to a batting cage for a more advanced, challenging drill. Begin by placing a batting tee at home plate. Have hitters try to drive the ball in the air to the very back part of the cage. Let each player take 10 swings and record the results. Remember, the ball must reach the back of the cage in the air without touching any other part of the cage. Sounds easy? It's not. Only a near-perfect or perfect swing will produce the desired result. This is a great drill for producing the ideal, level-to-slightly-descending swing path every hitter should strive for. Also, the ball must be contacted in the right spot to produce enough backspin to carry it to the back of the cage. Later, change the drill by swinging at soft toss or underhand pitches. Have the pitcher kneel *behind* an L-screen at a position diagonal to the plate and about 12 to 15 feet away. The hitters will learn to keep their hands inside the ball and wait until the pitch gets to the ideal position for driving it back through the middle.

17

BUNT INTO THE BUCKET

Bunting should be part of any team's basic game plan, particularly at the youth level. Sacrifice bunting, giving up an out to advance a runner or runners, is the ultimate act of teamwork. Bunting for a base hit, or "drag bunting," adds a valuable weapon to any player's offensive arsenal. Here's a fun game that will help your players become better bunters.

How It's Done

Place two five-gallon buckets in fair territory approximately 12 feet away from the nearest point of home plate—one about three feet from the third baseline and the other about three feet from the first baseline—with the openings facing home plate. The game is played by giving each player nine sacrifice bunt attempts, divided into three rounds of three bunts each. Each player will receive a score based on his proficiency: He gets three points for any ball that rolls into a bucket and two points for any ball bunted fair that misses a bucket but does not go past its opening; he loses one point for a foul ball, a ball bunted higher than four feet into the air, a bunt and miss, or a called strike. Any ball bunted fair between a bucket and the foul line is a "do over," because you don't want the player being too fine with a sacrifice bunt. A player may call his shot (declare before the pitch into which bucket he will bunt the ball) to receive a bonus of three points. The player with the most points at the end of the three rounds is declared the winner. Once your players have become competent at the sacrifice bunt, have them try drag bunting to make the game more challenging.

Purpose

Bunting is a skill that's often neglected, but it's one that should be practiced right from the start. First, a sacrifice bunt is the ultimate act of selflessness. The player is giving himself up to advance the greater interests of the team. Bunting helps to reinforce the idea that each player is only a small part of something bigger. Second, because bunting requires bat control, players will learn the hand-eye coordination and dexterity necessary in many other parts of

If the batter calls his shot and bunts the ball into the bucket, an additional three bonus points are awarded.

the game, including the full swing. They'll also improve their ability to catch a thrown ball, because good bunting is little more than "catching" the ball with the bat—and if you can catch the ball with a bat, you certainly can catch it with a glove. Third, a player who develops a real aptitude for bunting is helping to build an identity for himself in the game. It gives a kid something to be proud of.

This game provides a psychological benefit, too. It helps players overcome their fear of being hit by a pitched ball, because bunting requires courage. The hitter has to put the bat out in front of him, over the plate and into the path of the pitch, to get a good bunt down, and he can't do that if he's afraid of the ball. The game will also help you, the coach, know which players you can count on to get a bunt down at a crucial point in the game.

GAME TIP

Good bat position is imperative for successful bunting. The hitter must first get the bat to a position at the top of the strike zone. This way he knows that anything above bat-level is a ball, and it's easier to move the bat down to the ball than it is to move it up. Next, he must make sure the barrel of the bat is in fair territory as he awaits the pitch. This will help him keep the bunt fair, because the first bounce will happen in fair territory, where the field is better manicured, even if he bunts the ball straight down. If he's sacrificing, he has to wait to see the ball down on the ground before he starts running. If he leaves the batter's box prematurely and is struck by a fair ball, he's out.

18

PEPPER

Every player should spend significant time working on bat control. There is always a spot for a guy who can handle the bat. A player may be asked to hit behind the runner on the hit-and-run play; hit the ball into the air to drive home a runner from third; or pull the ball behind the runner to advance him to the next base. A big swing-and-miss may draw oohs and aahs from the crowd, but a strikeout does nothing for the team. The name of the game is to *put the ball in play*. The best game for learning bat control is called Pepper, and it has been around almost as long as baseball itself.

How It's Done

Pepper can be played by as few as two players or as many as six. I recommend playing it with four players, one batter and three fielders. The fielders stand side by side, about six feet apart, in a line approximately 20 feet from the batter and facing him. The game begins when a fielder pitches a ball to the batter. The batter, who has choked up on the bat an inch or two, takes a short, controlled swing at the ball, directing it on the ground to one of the fielders. The ball is then pitched back to the hitter, and the process is repeated. The batter must swing at every pitch, no matter how bad,

The game of Pepper develops hand-to-eye coordination and bat control. Players choke up on the bat and take a short, level swing.

and he must attempt to direct his hit to a particular fielder. Each batter continues until he swings and misses twice or until one of the fielders catches a hit ball before it touches the ground, at which time that fielder exchanges places with the batter. Have the hitters monitor their progress by counting how many balls they can hit before being replaced.

Purpose

In Pepper, batters almost never strike out. Why? Because the batter's swing is controlled—he isn't trying to kill the ball. Another reason is that he lets the ball get to him, meaning he gets to see it longer. He isn't trying to pull the ball. This is the art of bat control, of making consistent contact. Pepper will show players how easy it is to hit the ball every time. If they take to the game what they learn in Pepper (that is, seeing the ball longer; using a short, controlled swing; hitting the top of the ball; using the entire field), they will immediately become better hitters and more valuable players.

FUNDAMENTAL TIP

Another lesson a player can learn from Pepper is that choking up on the bat, or moving his hands up the handle away from the knob, shortens his swing and gives him more bat control. Hitters fear that choking up will rob them of power. Wrong! Power is largely a product of bat speed and square contact. By choking up, they will increase bat speed and improve bat control, which means they will swing faster and make more consistent contact, and that translates into power. Don't believe it? Watch Barry Bonds. For more than a decade, Bonds has been one of the most consistent home run hitters in baseball, and he chokes up at least an inch or two for every at-bat. He trades length for bat speed, and the results speak for themselves. Teach your players to choke up. It's one of the smartest things any hitter can do.

19

CALL-YOUR-SHOT
BATTING PRACTICE

A good friend of mine who is a former major-league player told me about an interesting batting practice routine used by his former teammate, Hall of Famer Eddie Murray. My friend said that during batting practice Murray would often choose very precise targets, such as the first base bag and the third base bag, which he would then attempt to hit with a batted ball. Choosing such tiny targets forced him to focus intensely on controlling his bat. By focusing on bat control, Murray was preparing himself for any type of situational hitting he might face in the game. While it isn't reasonable to expect young players to control the bat as well as Eddie Murray, there is a great batting practice game you can play that will focus their attention on hitting the ball to targeted locations. Just as in the popular basketball game H-O-R-S-E, the players get to call their own shots.

How It's Done

Set up for standard batting practice, with you (the coach) pitching and each of the other defensive positions filled. During the first

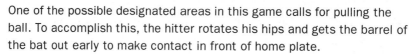

One of the possible designated areas in this game calls for pulling the ball. To accomplish this, the hitter rotates his hips and gets the barrel of the bat out early to make contact in front of home plate.

round of batting practice, each player gets seven swings and may hit the ball to any part of the field. The second round becomes a game in which the hitter must declare (before swinging) where he plans to hit the ball: pull, up the middle, opposite field. He gets three swings to hit the ball into his designated area. As long as the batter successfully calls his shots, he stays at the plate. He may not call his shot to the same area twice in a row. If he fails to hit the ball into his designated area, he switches positions with one of the fielders. For the third round of batting practice, the hitter is afforded only one swing to hit the ball to his designated area.

Purpose

The primary purpose of this game is to help players develop bat control, the ability to manipulate the bat and their hands so they can use all parts of the field. They will also learn how to let the ball get deeper into the strike zone, because that is the only way to consistently hit it to the opposite field (when that is their designated area).

Letting the ball get deeper into the zone affords the hitter a longer look at the pitch. This is an excellent tactic anytime, but especially when he's behind in the count. Also, the ability to control the bat is paramount for successful situational hitting. For example, presented with a runner on second and no outs, it is the batter's job to hit the ball to the right side of the field to advance the runner to third. Bat control can and does win games in big ways and small ones.

Choking up an inch or two shortens the bat, increases bat speed, and improves bat control.

A bonus of this game is that the fielders get to work on their defense by playing the ball live off the bat. This simulates game conditions better than infield practice does.

PRACTICE TIP

When working to improve bat control, the batting practice pitcher is crucial. He must be able to pitch strikes to both the inside and outside parts of the strike zone. A pitcher with precise control can help hitters by feeding them balls that are easier to hit to designated areas. For example, it is much easier to pull an inside pitch, and it is easier to hit an outside pitch to the opposite field. These "friendly" pitches will help the hitter gain confidence in his ability to hit the ball to all fields. Later, when hitters have become more adept at controlling the bat, the pitcher should challenge them with more difficult pitches. He should ask them to hit the ball to the opposite field, then make it difficult by throwing pitches to the inside part of the strike zone. When a hitter can, on demand, pull an outside pitch and take an inside pitch to the opposite field, he has become a master of the art of bat control.

20

NAME THAT COLOR

When assessing a hitter's technique, it is natural for coaches to focus on things such as stance, posture, stride, swing, and follow-through. But there is another crucial factor in hitting that doesn't always receive the attention it deserves: the hitter's ability to pick the ball up out of the pitcher's hand and to focus on it intensely as it travels to the hitting zone. Although all hitters can see the ball, some see it better than others. No one hits well what they don't see well. Fortunately, like all other important baseball skills, you can improve your players' vision through practice. I recommend a game called Name That Color.

How It's Done

This game involves the use of four baseballs, each with one quarter of its surface painted: One ball is red, one is blue, another is green, and the last is yellow. You (the coach) pitch batting practice with the colored balls, and the hitters must identify as quickly as possible the color on the ball, then swing and hit it. Ask one of the other coaches to use a stopwatch to record how quickly the players correctly identify the color on each ball. You can make this into a game by giving points for quick, accurate color identification and bonus points for hitting the ball hard.

Draw or paint a different color dot (red, blue, green, and yellow) on each of four baseballs. As the ball is released, the hitter calls out the color of the ball thrown. The quicker the call, the greater number of points awarded.

Purpose

This game will help hitters focus their vision better, to pick the ball up right out of the pitcher's hand. By asking the hitter to not only identify the color, but to hit the ball as well, you are forcing him to track the ball all the way into the hitting zone. This game will validate for the players the importance of vision in hitting. A hitter can have a great swing, but it's vision that tells him when the pitch is coming, how fast it is travelling, and where it is located.

FUNDAMENTAL TIP

Every coach and player has heard someone in the stands yell, "Keep your eyes on the ball." That's pretty obvious advice, to be sure, but when should the hitter start looking at the ball? Does he begin to focus as soon as the pitcher toes the rubber? Well, yes and no.

   The hitter should always observe what the pitcher is doing, directing his eyes in the pitcher's direction. But he shouldn't stare intently at the ball or the pitcher's glove for too long, because his eyes will become tired and he may lose his focus. Instead, the hitter should adopt what vision experts call a "soft center." That is, he should look at the pitcher, but not zero in on the ball or the pitcher's glove. He might pick out something behind the pitcher or simply look at the upper half of the pitcher's body. This way, the batter has a general awareness of the pitcher's movements but doesn't zero in on anything. Only when the pitcher gets to the point in his delivery when he swings his hand and the ball up to the release point should the batter go to a "hard focus." At this point, he devotes 100 percent of his attention and focus to seeing the ball come out of the pitcher's hand and tracking its path to the plate.

21

ONE-HANDED HACKS

In general, the hands work as a single unit when swinging the bat. But when broken down, each hand has a specific purpose in the swing. The bottom hand (the left hand for right-handed hitters) starts the swing by pulling the bat forward and down toward the ball. The top hand then takes over and fires the barrel at the ball moments before it enters the hitting zone. To hit the ball with authority, each hand must carry out its function at the proper time.

You may have heard of "pull hitters," who acquire this title because they have a top-hand dominant swing. Their top hand controls the swing from the get-go, and the barrel of the bat fires through the hitting zone prematurely. Their wrists roll too soon. Because the barrel of the bat is out in front of home plate at the point of contact, balls are hit to the pull side. "Inside-out hitters" are exactly the opposite. In this case, the bottom hand dominates the entire swing, and the top hand fires too late. The bat is first pulled forward and then slices or cuts at the ball. Because the barrel trails the hands at contact, balls are invariably hit to the opposite field. One-Handed Hacks will allow hitters to learn the role of each hand—by hand—and how it should contribute to a fundamentally sound swing.

How It's Done

Using the side of a batting cage net or a fence, set up the hitter for soft tosses. To do this, the feeder rests on one knee and lightly

The batter chokes up so his hand grips the bat at the top of the handle. He uses his hand, wrist, and forearm to fire the barrel directly to the ball.

tosses balls aimed waist-high and slightly in front of the hitter. The hitter takes his stance and positions himself to hit balls directly into the net.

For this drill, the hitter chokes way up on the bat, moving his top hand just above the grip on an aluminum bat. He takes his bottom hand off the bat. To avoid using other parts of his body (such as his shoulders and back) to control and swing the bat, he should try using a lighter bat. It will make things a little easier for him. Holding the bat in his customary stance position, the hitter takes swings at flipped balls using just his top hand. Make sure he keeps the barrel up and fires it directly at the ball. A key point to this drill is to get batters to concentrate on using just their wrist and forearm to swing the bat. They should not use their shoulder to power the swing; this creates a long swing path to the ball. Have them think about firing the bat directly to the ball using a short, compact stroke. See how many consecutive line drives each batter is able to hit into the net.

Now the batter switches hands to work on his lead arm. This is a little more difficult and takes practice to get used to. He holds the bat above the handle with his bottom hand and takes his top hand off the bat. As the feeder tosses the ball, the batter should hit the ball squarely and drive through it. Again, he should use his wrist and forearm to fuel his swing, stay short to the ball, and keep the barrel of the bat up. The tendency is to let the barrel dip, but it should be at or slightly above the baseball as it makes contact.

Purpose

Learning the individual roles of the top and bottom hands allows hitters to feel what each should contribute. To hit the ball successfully in this drill, they must fire the barrel directly to the ball. This promotes a short, quick swing—a swing that produces optimal results. Pull hitters and inside-out hitters should use this drill regularly. It will help them develop a more balanced swing that strikes the ball squarely.

GAME TIP

There are times during a baseball game when hitters need to adjust their swing to accomplish what's needed for the specific situation. With a runner on second base and nobody out, it's the batter's job to hit the ball to the right side of second base and advance the runner to third. A runner on third base with one out can score on a fly ball, ground ball, or wild pitch.

A right-handed hitter should concentrate on two things to get the job done. First, he should let the ball travel deep into the hitting zone. This enables him to contact the ball near the back of home plate, which produces a hit to the right side of the infield. Second, he should allow his lead arm to dominate the swing, so the barrel stays back. When the top hand fires early, the angle of the bat sends balls to the left side of the infield. The barrel should trail the batter's hands so he hits balls to the right side of the infield.

A left-handed hitter must produce the same results by making the opposite adjustments. He needs to get the swing started early so contact is made out in front of home plate and the balls will be pulled. He also needs to roll his top hand over early so the barrel angle sends the ball to the right side of the infield.

This is an advanced hitting skill that can be learned very early. During a game, have the hitter try at least once to move a runner over. If he fouls the pitch off or swings through it, tell him he can swing away for the rest of his at-bat.

22

SHORT-FIELD BATTING PRACTICE

Legendary Hall of Famer Reggie Jackson once remarked after he lined out to the second baseman to end a late-inning Yankees rally, "You can only hit the ball hard; you can't direct the ball to an open area." To a large extent, this is true. A batter should concentrate first and foremost on choosing a pitch he can handle and then hitting that pitch as hard as he can. This is especially true when an extra base hit is needed to score two or more base runners.

However, some situations do call for directing batted balls to specific parts of the field. For example, with a runner on second base with no one out, the batter should try to advance the runner to third. He can do this by hitting a ground ball to the right side of the diamond or even a deep fly ball to right field. This calls for bat control. When the defense pulls its infield in to cut off a run at home plate, the batter can shoot the ball on the ground to either side of the field through the drawn-in infield. Short-Field Batting Practice is one way to develop the skill of directing balls to designated parts of the field.

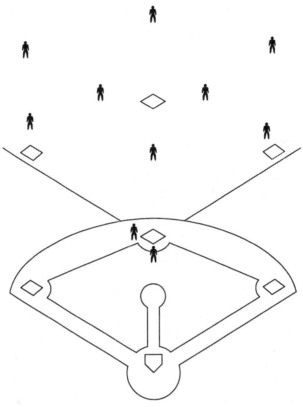

Take team batting practice using second base as home plate. Each swing should have a purpose, but any ball hit over the fence counts against the batter.

How It's Done

Set up a diamond behind second base, using second base as home plate. Place fielders at each position and designate three players as the hitters. One player bats and the other two retrieve foul tips that the catcher doesn't catch. Give each batter seven pitches. Instruct them to hit ground balls through holes in the infield: three between the first baseman and second baseman, three up the middle between the shortstop and second baseman, and one between the shortstop and third baseman. Score each batter's turn, giving two points for each ground ball that goes through the designated areas. Deduct one point for any ball hit into the air, two points for any ball hit in the air and caught, and three points for any ball hit over the fence. Rotate the hitters. When the first hitter is finished with his seven swings, he moves to right field, then center field, left field, third base, and so on until he's played all the positions except pitcher and catcher. The first baseman joins the other two hitters at home plate. Tally the points and declare a winner after two complete rounds.

Purpose

The object of this game is to teach players how to direct the ball toward designated areas of the field, to hit the ball on the ground, and to know the value of a well-placed hit. By practicing closer to the outfield fence, you will reinforce the necessity of hitting the ball on the ground—any ball that is lifted will fly over the fence.

COACHING TIP

Harry Walker, the famous major-league batting instructor, emphasized bat control when he taught hitting. According to Walker, "There is always a place on any team, anywhere, for a guy who can handle the bat. For the greatest degree of bat control, however, the middle finger joints of both hands should be roughly aligned. This position affords one the greatest wrist freedom. One other thing to remember: The fingers do more holding than the palms, just as in the case of a golfer and his club."

To hit a ball to the opposite field, the batter needs to use an "inside-out" swing, meaning the lead arm dominates his stroke. First, have your players choke the grip an inch or so. Instruct them to drag the barrel of the bat through the strike zone, with their hands leading the barrel and remaining in the position of palm up (top hand), palm down (bottom hand) on contact. Give them the image of letting the ball travel deep into the strike zone (thus making contact toward the back of the plate). Their hips should open so their belly button faces right center field and their shoulders rotate less than 180 degrees. Most important swing thought: The barrel trails the hands at contact.

PART 4 BASERUNNING

23

DON'T BREAK THE EGG

Whacking a single or legging out a double is a great feeling. However, the scoreboard doesn't change until a player crosses home plate. Proper baserunning can make all the difference. Baserunning is one of least scrutinized aspects of the game but is essential to a player's or team's success.

And sliding is a critical element to baserunning. Most kids enjoy sliding but often slide incorrectly. One of the most common errors is that they use their hands to brace their fall (or slide). This is the cause of many wrist injuries suffered in youth baseball. Players must be taught the proper technique to sliding; that is, to throw their hands up in the air as they land on their rear end. To do this, try incorporating Don't Break the Egg into your practice routine.

How It's Done

Dress each player in a pair of nylon pants. (This drill is going to produce some major grass stains.) Take a hose and wet down a 10-foot area in the outfield grass, and place cones to indicate where the wet grass begins and ends. Put a flat base or baseball glove on the ground to give players their sliding destination. Line the players up so they have to run approximately 30 to 40 feet before reaching the wet grass.

Hand the player two eggs and have him hold one in each hand.

Hand the first runner two eggs. He must hold the eggs in his hands from the time he starts running straight through the slide. The object is to execute the slide while keeping both eggs intact. If the runner allows his hands to contact the ground during the slide,

As the player starts his slide, his hands and arms raise up toward the sky. This keeps his hands (and eggs) safe.

the eggs will break. If he throws his hands up in the air as he's supposed to, the eggs will survive the exercise. On your call, the runner sprints toward the wet grass and slides feet first. Each player should slide four to six times.

To make this a game, divide the players into two teams. Give each team two eggs. One by one, the players take off for the base and slide in hard. The team that goes the longest without breaking *both* eggs wins.

Make sure the clever ones don't start packing hard-boiled eggs in their equipment bags.

Purpose

The object of this drill is to teach kids the proper way to slide. Ripped palms, jammed thumbs, and sprained wrists occur frequently because they fail to throw their hands upward when they should. By practicing on a softer surface (wet grass), players slide more aggressively. Instead of worrying about cuts and scrapes they might get from a harder surface, they can concentrate on the fundamental skills of sliding. Holding the eggs while running will train them to relieve tension in their hands. Young players tend to make a fist and tense up while sprinting, and tension diminishes running speed. Holding the eggs will force the player to relax his hands or end up with egg on them.

GAME TIP

When players are involved in a close play at first base, they sometimes make the mistake of sliding headfirst into the bag. Whether they observed this tactic on television or at a high school or college game, they must be told that it is ineffective and should not be practiced.

Sliding headfirst into first base adds precious time to the race to the bag. Think about it. Have you ever seen a world-class sprinter like Donovan Bailey, Michael Johnson, or Maurice Green dive across the finish line? No, because the fastest way to cross the finish line is to continue running through it. The same holds true for running to first base. To dive into first base, the runner must slow down to lower his body and then dive. His chances of being called safe are greatly reduced. The only time to consider sliding is if the throw from the infielder is off-line and the runner is attempting to avoid a tag.

Another reason not to slide headfirst into first base is the risk of injury. The runner can jam his thumb, sprain his wrist, injure his shoulder, and so on. During the 1999 play-offs, Cleveland Indians center fielder Kenny Lofton dislocated his shoulder sliding headfirst into first base. He was out for the rest of the series, and his shoulder required surgery during the off-season. Tell your players to stay on their feet when running to first base. It's the fastest and safest way to travel.

24

RELAY RACE

Every player can improve his baserunning. Unfortunately, young players rarely practice this. Slow runners commonly shy away from working at this aspect of their game because they accept it as a weakness and consider the situation hopeless. Fast runners fail to practice because they believe their speed automatically makes them good base runnners. This couldn't be further from the truth.

There are a number of ways to reduce time and increase speed on the base paths, including executing proper turns, cutting down angles, anticipating defensive errors, and using proper running form. A fast runner, for example, who makes a wide turn around third base is only as effective as a mediocre runner who executes a good turn. Those close plays at the plate can become safe calls if you make baserunning drills part of each practice. Here is a game that forces players to concentrate on improving their skills in this area.

How It's Done

Divide the team in half to form Teams A and B. Place the players from Team A at home plate and those from Team B at second. Before the race begins, demonstrate the correct path to run around

At your signal, the first runner for each team starts running.

Once the runner has circled the bases, he passes the ball off to the next runner, who is not permitted to leave the base until he's handed the ball.

the bases, executing proper form and turns. Set up cones (gloves or hats work just as well) to mark points that runners should stay within while making turns.

The race is conducted as follows: The first runner for each team is given a ball. On your signal, both runners start to run. They circle the bases just as they would in a game. As soon as each player completes one lap around the bases, the ball is passed to the next player on that team. The ball must be handed off; it cannot be tossed or rolled to a teammate. Passing the ball through the air means immediate disqualification.

The race continues until all the runners have circled the bases. Each player should finish where he started. The first team to finish wins the race. The winning team gets to gloat, while the losers must pay a price you set.

Purpose

Because it's a race (and kids love relay races), players will run at top speed. This simulates the pace they'll run during a game. Practicing proper turns, correct running form, and cutting angles only serves a purpose if players are running at 100 percent effort.

They will quickly recognize that a wide turn increases their running time. They'll soon learn to tighten up their angles as they approach and round each base. This positive adjustment will eventually translate into game action, improving the manner in which they circle the bases.

GAME TIP

Players generally know when their batted balls will get through the infield and into the outfield. When this happens, they should immediately set their sights on second base. Running aggressively out of the batter's box can turn a single into a double.

Once the ball finds a hole in the infield, the hitter (now the runner) bows out to the foul territory side of the first baseline. He makes a gradual turn outward. About two-thirds of the way down the line, he makes a gradual turn back inward so that when he touches first base, his momentum is heading toward second base.

Even if the hit is a sure single off the bat, runners should make a strong turn toward second base as if they were going for a double. If the outfielder fields the ball cleanly, the runner can stop (about one-third of the way to second base) and retreat to first base. If the outfielder bobbles the ball or misses it, the runner can continue to second (and possibly third) without breaking stride.

Runners often mistakenly run straight down the first baseline when they get a hit. This makes it very difficult to advance to second base. They'll be forced to slow down so they can turn their body toward second base, creating a loss of momentum. If they don't slow down, they will then make a wide turn out toward right field before gaining control and continuing their run toward second base. This adds to the time it takes to arrive at second base. A few fractions of a second can mean the difference between sliding in safely and being thrown out. Runners should make a gradual turn right out of the box.

PART 5 TEAM GAMES

25

SANDLOT GAME

Like most middle-aged people who played baseball as a kid, I recall with great fondness the pickup games my friends and I played whenever we didn't have a practice or game scheduled. We brought our own bats and balls, chose teams, created our own line-ups, called close plays out or safe, and played as many innings as we wanted. We did all this without any help from adults, and in the process we learned how to play the game the old-fashioned way: through trial and error. Although the sandlot pickup game is mostly a thing of the past—a victim of suburban life and myriad other recreational choices—I believe it is still the purest form of baseball and the best way for a kid to learn the game. I believe every coach should include it in his practice schedule.

How It's Done

You bring all the equipment—bats, balls, catcher's gear, etc.—then get out of the way. Allow the players to choose sides and play a game on their own, including making any special rules. (For example, there may not be enough players to field two complete teams, meaning that some positions must be left vacant.) You stick around only to make certain that they're safe. Do not invite parents to this game; *this is players only*. Resist the temptation to coach or intercede in disputes.

Purpose

Your goal is to help your players gain a true appreciation for baseball as a *game*, without criticism or fine-tuning of their technique. The hope is that they'll enjoy themselves enough to want to do it again and again. This is how the nuances of the game are best learned, how you develop instinct. Through trial and error, without any pressure from adults, kids will discover what works and doesn't work, much as they do with computer games. Those who enjoy playing on their own, outside of structured practices and games, will become better, more confident players. They'll also learn about organization, leadership, honesty (they'll be the umpires, too), and friendly competition, all while gaining a sense of independence. As a bonus, everyone over 40 will love you for reintroducing sandlot baseball into your community.

By organizing and proctoring their own games, kids develop valuable skills like leadership and honesty.

GAME TIP

As a coach, it is important to remember that the players must not value baseball according to their batting average, their strikeouts, or the number of home runs they hit. For kids, the true value in the youth baseball experience comes from socializing with their friends and improving their skills. They don't sign up for baseball so they can be coached by an adult. They sign up to play a game with other kids. Set aside some time for them to play by themselves. With all due respect, they won't miss you that much.

26

EVERYBODY TOUCH IT

There are few things more rewarding for coaches than watching your players figure something out on their own, whether it be how much of a lead to take, where to position themselves on defense, or what type of approach to use at the plate. As much as possible, we should encourage kids to figure things out for themselves, especially the strategic and tactical parts of the game. After all, you won't be standing next to them during game situations. Toward that end, I suggest Everybody Touch It as a game that will encourage original thinking by all the participants, both hitters and fielders.

How It's Done

Divide the team into two squads, one in the field and one at bat. The defense may position its players in any formation. The game begins when the ball is pitched to the batter. Once the batter puts the ball into play, he continues to run the bases until each player in the field has touched the ball and it is relayed back to the pitcher. The batter may run around the bases twice or more! The offensive team's score is the total number of bases accumulated by all its play-

Once the batter strikes the ball, he sprints around the bases to touch as many bases as he can before the ball is thrown back to the pitcher.

ers. Once each player has batted and run the bases, the teams switch sides. The team with the highest number of bases wins the game.

Purpose

The benefits of this game are many. On offense, bat control will allow batters to hit the ball in a direction that will force the defense to spend significant time getting the ball to each player. Also, the offensive players will learn to use proper baserunning technique (that is, touching the corner of each base with the proper foot and making a quick, hard turn toward the next base) to accumulate the most bases. Also, running the bases long and hard will improve the cardiovascular condition of all players.

On defense, players will learn the value of working together to position themselves wisely and finding the best method for getting every player to touch the ball in the shortest amount of time. The defensive players will also be learning the best relay techniques, involving strong, accurate throws and quickly transferring the ball from glove to throwing hand. As a bonus, all the players will subconsciously learn how to function under the pressure of competition.

One method of getting each player to touch the ball is to line up and pass the ball backward through the legs. The defense forms a line behind the player who reaches the ball first and then passes the ball along the ground.

GAME TIP

One thing that's amazing about baseball is the number of close plays that occur in nearly every game. It seems like there are always a couple of "bang-bang" plays at first and a close tag play or two at the other bases. Often, these plays are the difference between a hit and an out, between winning and losing. Is it luck? No. Baserunning skill has much to do with who's out and who's safe; it's a critical part of the game. Four simple lessons on baserunning should be learned by every young player:

1. Always run as hard as you can between bases.
2. As much as possible, run in a straight line, making your turns as tight as possible.
3. When rounding any base, always touch the inside corner of the bag with your body leaning in the direction of the next base.
4. When rounding a base, use your left foot to touch the inside corner of the bag, because this creates a forward lean toward the next base, enabling you to travel on a straighter line. One caution: You should never slow down just so you can touch the base with your left foot.

Have your players practice these techniques until they become second nature.

27

SEVEN POSITIONS

s a kid, I remember that the coach always seemed to put our least talented player in right field. Why? I'm not sure, because right field is a very important position and arguably the most difficult outfield position to play. The most talented kids played shortstop and pitcher, and the rest of the positions were filled in a seemingly random manner. I know there were many kids who wished for an opportunity to play different positions—sometimes to show the coach what they could do, other times just to see what those positions were like. In baseball, like most other things, variety is the spice. I believe kids enjoy the game more if they have a chance to experience more and different things. Try the game Seven Positions as a way to let kids live out some of their fantasies. As a bonus, you might just find that new shortstop you've been looking for.

How It's Done

Divide the team into two squads and play a seven-inning practice game. The pitchers and catchers play their normal positions throughout, but each of the other players switch positions each inning, playing a total of seven positions during the game. After

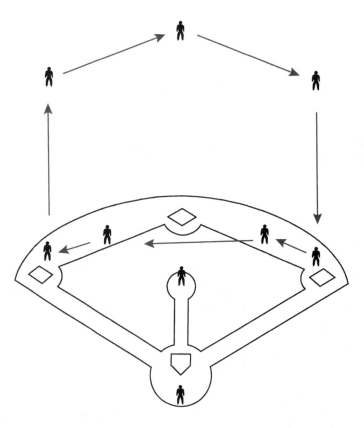

Each player rotates to a different position at the start of a new inning.

the first inning, the first baseman goes to second base, the second baseman to shortstop, the shortstop to third base, the third baseman to left field, the left fielder to center field, the center fielder to right field, and the right fielder to first base. After each inning, the players rotate positions in the same manner.

Purpose

This game allows your players to demonstrate their skills all over the field, and it affords you an opportunity to evaluate players at different positions. Players also gain a new appreciation for the challenges that each position presents. For example, the left fielder who has been champing at the bit to show his stuff at shortstop may quickly learn that the demands of the position require skills he doesn't yet possess. At the same time, the second baseman who has been struggling at that position may find that his skills are better suited for an outfield position. Mostly, though, this game is played for fun, to break up the routine of practice.

GAME TIP

The more positions a player can play, the more valuable he becomes to the team and the more flexibility you have as a coach. One example of this is Melvin Mora, a major-league player for the Baltimore Orioles. During his career, Mora has played all the outfield positions and all the infield positions except first base. He is not excellent at any one position, but he is competent at many, and it is for that reason that he remains in the major leagues. His value lies in his versatility. Maybe there's a kid like that on your team.

28

THE FUNGO GAME

Coaches and players love to play intrasquad games. Players love them because the conditions are so similar to real games, and coaches love them because their players get to practice all their baseball skills simultaneously. The problem with intrasquad games, though, is pitching: There's never enough of it. And if one of the pitchers struggles with his control, the game really drags and the kids lose interest. There is a way, however, to guarantee maximum value from your intrasquad games: Play what I call The Fungo Game.

How It's Done

Position nine players in the field on defense; the rest are the offense. Play begins when the pitcher simulates a pitch. The batter then tosses a ball to himself and hits it into the field of play. This is called fungo hitting. The rest of the game is played exactly like a regulation baseball game, except that each time a batter is put out, he exchanges places with a defensive player. Also, no batter may hit the ball to the same location in two consecutive at-bats.

Keep track of which batter makes the fewest outs and scores the most runs. Every batter gets a minimum of four at-bats during the

With the catcher standing to the side, the batter throws the ball up to himself and whacks it into play. No batter may hit the ball to the same location in two consecutive at-bats.

game. You want to encourage the players to hit hard ground balls and line drives. You may choose to emphasize this point by declaring that any fly ball caught in the air counts as two outs against the batter's total. Some players may have difficulty getting the hang of throwing the ball up and hitting it. You may allow these players to use a tee until they become more proficient at fungo hitting.

Purpose

This game helps players develop virtually every important baseball skill: fielding, baserunning, hitting, and strategic and tactical decision making. And as an added bonus, the game moves quickly. You can get plenty of at-bats for all the players in half the time it would take to play a game with live pitching.

Fungo batting definitely improves bat control. If the batter wants to hit the ball hard on the ground, the bat must follow a level or slightly descending path to the ball. That's the ideal swing path for successful hitting. If he wants to pull the ball, he must get his bat out in front of home plate. If he wants to hit the ball to the opposite field, he must let the ball get deeper into the hitting zone.

Defensive players will get plenty of action, too, because the ball is put into play on every "pitch." On defense, if a player closely watches the toss of the ball, the batter's body movement, and the bat angle, he'll be able to read where the ball is likely to go, letting him get a good jump on the ball. There's no standing around waiting for the pitcher to throw a strike or for the batter to make contact.

TRY THIS

The first key to hitting for a high average is to make consistent contact. You can't bat over .300 if you don't put the ball into play nearly all the time. The second key is to translate that consistent contact into line drives and hard ground balls. Let's face it, most baseball players can't regularly hit long, majestic fly balls over the fence, so their success is dependent on singles and doubles. Tony Gwynn, for example, is a great hitter who has fashioned his success out of consistently hitting the ball down and hard. Gwynn is not a power hitter, but he regularly posts a .300 batting average. He hits line drives and ground balls to all parts of the field, but particularly to the opposite field. By letting the ball get deeper into the hitting zone, he sees the ball longer and puts himself into position to hit down and through it—a sure recipe for line drives and hard ground balls. Every young hitter's mantra should be "Down and Hard."

29

2–1 COUNT SCRIMMAGE

Baseball games can proceed at a slow pace, especially at youth levels. Regardless, practice games must be incorporated in training sessions because it's the only way players will develop instinct and a sufficient comfort level for playing the game. The 2–1 Count Scrimmage game is the perfect remedy. It allows kids to play games, but at a quick pace.

How It's Done

Divide the squad into two evenly matched teams and play an intrasquad game. Every batter starts with a 2–1 count. If the first pitch is a strike, the count suddenly moves to 2–2. A ball thrown out of the strike zone runs the count to 3–1. The pitcher is immediately in danger of walking the batter.

Instead of playing a predetermined number of innings, set a time limit for the game and continue until time expires. You'll be surprised at the number of innings the squad will play in the allotted time.

Purpose

Because of the advanced count, pitchers must be aggressive throwing strikes, and the hitters are compelled to swing the bat. With four balls to work with, pitchers often fail to concentrate early in the count. They feel they have some breathing room and quickly fall behind in the count. Hitters, who have three strikes to work with, frequently take a more passive approach at the plate. They keep the bat on their shoulder early on and quickly find themselves in a hole.

This game forces pitchers to throw strikes immediately and hitters to swing the bat. Batted balls are put into play at an accelerated rate, which allows the defense to field more balls in game situations.

By starting with a 2–1 count, the concentration and aggression level of the hitter and pitcher are intensified.

The pace of the game is very quick. The hitters get more at-bats, and the pitchers face more hitters. The defense stays on their toes, which leads to sharper defensive play. To make the game move even faster, start every batter with a 2–2 count.

FUNDAMENTAL TIP

Drills teach proper fundamentals and develop muscle memory in baseball players. Both are essential to improving performance. What drills fail to teach is instinct. Instinct is not a trait that is noticeable in batting practice; it doesn't show up on radar guns, nor is it displayed on a stopwatch. Instinct is an often-unnoticed characteristic, but it's extremely valuable to a baseball player and his teammates.

What is instinct? Taking an extra base can be instinctual. As a base runner, knowing immediately that a batted ball will drop between outfielders is instinctual. Bobbling a ball in the field and knowing whether you still have a play is instinctual. These are all examples of subconscious knowledge gained through playing games.

How do you help your players develop instinct? Instinct comes from repetition in gamelike circumstances. Playing as many games as possible instills instinct in players. This is especially true when the games are unsupervised (see Sandlot Game). Players will learn the nuances of the game through trial and error. They'll learn when to take risks and when to play it safe. Drills certainly hold merit in baseball practice, but there is no substitute for live-action games.

30

KIDS VERSUS PARENTS

This book is about making baseball more fun for kids. Parents and their children often need to be reminded that baseball is a *game* and having fun should be the focal point. Too much emphasis is placed on statistics, wins, and losses, which diminishes the pure enjoyment of the game.

Baseball, more than any other sport, is a game that must be played in a relaxed manner in order to play efficiently. It is unique from other mainstream sports such as football, soccer, basketball, and hockey in that maximum effort doesn't always produce the sought-after results. Swinging the bat as hard as possible diminishes bat speed and power and decreases the chance of making contact. Throwing a pitch as hard as possible reduces velocity and control. Exerting strenuous physical effort or suffering from mental anguish adversely affects player performance. More often than not, this is caused by unnecessary pressure placed on the child by others. Kids must learn to stay relaxed and enjoy themselves. Only then will they have the opportunity to achieve optimum results.

A game of Kids Versus Parents is a refreshing way to spend a practice. Everyone participating will not only have a great time, but the parents will quickly learn that the game is not as easy as it appears from the stands.

How It's Done

Parents of all children on the team must attend baseball practice. They can either dust off an old glove sitting in their garage or use their children's gloves. Once everyone has completed their stretching and loosening up, the kids are pitted against the parents in a just-for-fun game.

One of the coaches will pitch for both teams to control the speed of pitches and keep the game running smoothly. Every player on each team bats in the lineup. (If there are 14 kids on the team, all 14 are included in the batting order.) On defense, players and parents should rotate their positions throughout the game. For safety

Pitting the kids against the adults can be a fun experience for both groups. Use one of the various (softer) safety balls available on the market for this game. You don't want the parents getting hurt.

reasons, a rubber-coated, restricted-flight ball must be used when the parents are at bat.

Keep the game to four innings. Make sure everyone gets to bat at least once and plays at least two innings in the field. The winning team is served cookies and juice by the losing team.

Purpose

The main purpose of this game is to have some laughs and to reinforce the fact that baseball is just a game. Kids will get a kick out of seeing their parents swing the bat and chase fly balls. Conversely, at least one parent is bound to emerge as a Herculean-type figure in the eyes of the players.

The majority of the parents will quickly realize how difficult it is to hit, throw, and catch the ball. The next time they're in the stands watching a game, they may be a little less critical and more sympathetic when their child makes a mistake.

All in the Family

Many family trees have deep roots in major-league baseball. In addition to many notable father-son combinations like Bobby and Barry Bonds, Ken Griffey and Ken Griffey Jr., and Felipe and Moises Alou, there have been 360 brother combinations in the major leagues. Many of these brother combinations are very well known like Dom, Vince, and Joe DiMaggio and Sandy and Roberto Alomar. But no brothers had careers so close in comparison as Bob and Emil "Irish" Meusel.

Bob and Irish were very similar in their appearance and capabilities. During their major-league tenure, Irish had a career batting average of .310 compared to Bob's .309, both over 11 seasons. They played both left field and right field, where Bob recorded a .959

career fielding percentage compared to Irish's .958. Bob compiled 95 career triples, while Irish smacked 93. And Bob led the American League with 138 runs batted in (1925), while Irish led the same league with 125 in 1923.

The World Series from 1921 to 1923 featured Bob (of the Yankees) against older brother Irish (of the Giants). The fact that two brothers were squaring off in the Fall Classic gave additional luster to the season's biggest event. Before the 1921 Series, one writer summed up the pair: "Bob hits harder than Emil though he is not as consistent in garnering his hits. Bob also excels Emil as a thrower, but Emil is a more finished fielder. Bob is a left field hitter, and Emil often hits to right, so the play of 'Meusel flied to Meusel' may be repeated frequently during the Series."